AF252115

"There is an old proverb that says 'Thoughts disentangle themselves when passing over the lips and through the finger tips.' The 17:18 Series, which encourages us to actually write out the words of Scripture, will be a tremendous tool in putting that proverb into action in our daily lives. I am happy to commend this project."

–Jerry Bridges, a longtime staff member of the Navigators and author of *The Pursuit of Holiness*

"Several years ago I read an article about copying the Scriptures by hand. I tried it with the Pastoral Epistles, writing out all three books with a fountain pen in my journal, and found it a profitable exercise. I am glad to see this series of journals appear, and I hope they are widely used."

–Donald S. Whitney, Associate Professor of Biblical Spirituality, The Southern Baptist Theological Seminary, Louisville

The 17:18 Series

The Book of
Judges & Ruth

Joel R. Beeke and Rob Wynalda

This book belongs to:

____

Given by: ________________________

Date: ____________________________

Judges & Ruth

www.fullquiver5.com

Published by
Reformation Heritage Books
2965 Leonard St. NE
Grand Rapids, MI 49525
616-977-0889
email: orders@heritagebooks.org
website: www.heritagebooks.org

ISBN 978-1-60178-750-7

Cover Design: Bethany Sanderson and Steve Coy
Journible® Design: Rob Wynalda

Why the 17:18 series?

In Deuteronomy 17, Moses is leaving final instructions concerning the future of Israel. As a prophet of God, Moses foretells of when Israel will place a king over the nation (v. 14). In verses 16 & 17, he lists items that the king could not do as king. In verse 18, he transitions to what he should do as king.

The king is commanded not to simply acquire a copy of the law (the entire book of Deuteronomy) from the "scroll publishing house," but to handwrite his own copy of the law. The purpose of such a copy written by his own hand was so that:

* he would read it
* he would learn to fear the Lord
* he would obey the commands of God
* his heart would not become proud
* he would not turn to the right or the left from following the law (Prov. 4:27)
* also, his sons would serve in the kingdom after him (Deut. 17:19, 20).

Thirty-four hundred years later, educators are "discovering" that students who physically write out their notes by hand have a much greater retention rate than those who simply hear or visually read the information. Apparently, God knew this to be true for the kings of Israel also.

From such understanding came the conception of this series of books.

Have a great time writing and learning the Word of God,

Rob Wynalda
Romans 1:16

The Purpose of the Journible®

Engagement:

The Journible® is a profoundly simple attempt to aid a person's ability to engage the Word of God by slowing down the process of simply reading the text. The book is organized so that the "scribe" can slowly and thoughtfully engage the text while leaving plenty of room to write comments and questions about the text (Deuteronomy 17:18; Psalm 119; 2 Timothy 3:16, 17).

Legacy:

Journibles® provide a legacy to pass on from one generation to the next. The Journible® creates an opportunity for one generation to communicate in writing to the next generation their insights and personal applications of the text (Deuteronomy 6).

How to use this book

This book is organized so that the scribe (you) will handwrite your very own copy of Judges & Ruth. You will be writing the text of the Bible only on the right-hand page of the book. This should make for easier writing and also allows ample space on the left page of your open text to write your own notes and comments. From time to time a question or word will be lightly printed on the left page; these questions are to aid in further study, but should not interfere with your own notes and comments. This means that you are encouraged not only to write your own "copy" of the Bible, but also to write your own notes concerning the text.

Yes, we are setting aside our mass-produced Gutenberg Bibles and attempting to get back to the simple handwritten copy of the text.

Notes

(1) Who was Joshua? What was the significance of his death?

(2) What was indicated by Judah's leadership (see Gen. 49:8–12).

(3) What practical lessons can be learned from Judah and Simeon partnering together to defeat their enemies?

(6) What was the purpose of cutting off this pagan king's thumbs and big toes?

Judges 1:1-6

1

2

3

4

5

6

Notes

(7) Who controlled the city of Jerusalem at this time?

(8–10) What was the reason for Israel's fierce enmity against the Canaanites?

(12) Who was Caleb? What was his relationship to Joshua (see Num. 13–14)?

7

8

9

10

11

12

Notes

(16) Why did Israel show kindness to the Kenites (see Num. 10:29–32)?

13

14

15

16

17

Notes

(19) What is the paradox in this verse?

(21, 27–33) Why was Israel's failure to drive out from the land all the pagan nations problematic (see Josh. 6:17)?

18

19

20

21

22

23

24

Notes

25

26

27

28

29

30

Notes

(35) Why was forced labor a false victory for Israel?

31

32

33

34

35

36

Notes

(1) Who was the Angel of the Lord? What do His words in verses 1–3 reveal about His identity?

(3) What was the consequence of Israel's unfaithfulness to the covenant (see Josh. 23:11–13)?

(4–5) Was the weeping and sacrificing of the Israelites a sign of genuine repentance?

(6) What is the relationship between this account and the previous chapter, which begins with Joshua's death?

Judges 2:1-6

1

2

3

4

5

6

Notes

(7) How would the faithfulness manifested under Joshua have encouraged Israel to keep covenant with the Lord? How does it encourage you to do the same?

(8) What is indicated by Joshua's title "the servant of the Lord"? How are Joshua and his generation contrasted with the next generation of Israelites (see v. 10)?

(10) Why is it imperative for fathers to pass on the faith to their children (see Deut. 6:4–25)?

(12) What does it mean for the Lord to be provoked to anger? What is the wrath of God?

7

8

9

10

11

12

Notes

(13) What are the Baals and the Ashtaroth?

(14–15) How was the displeasure of God evidenced among the Israelites? What does this teach us about the devastating consequences of sin?

(16) What was God's purpose in raising up judges?

(17) Israel's idolatry is referred to as whoredom. How is idolatry a form of spiritual adultery (see Ezekiel 16)?

13

14

15

16

17

18

Notes

(20) What does God's anger reveal about His character?

Judges 2:19-23

19

20

21

22

23

Notes

(2) Why would it be important for this new generation to be trained for war?

(4) Why does God test Israel?
How does He still test believers today?

(6) How did intermarriage with the pagan nations prove to be a snare to the Israelites? What are the implications of this for Christian marriage?

Judges 3:1-6

1

2

3

4

5

6

Notes

(7) Why does the author frequently reference the sight of the Lord (see Heb. 4:13)?

(9) What is revealed about God in His response to the cry of Israel?

(10) What is the Spirit's role in the book of Judges (see Judg. 6:34; 11:29; 14:6)?

7

8

9

10

11

Notes

(12) Why would God strengthen a godless king like Eglon? How is God's sovereignty manifested here (see Prov. 21:1)?

(15) Why would the author mention that Ehud was left-handed?

12

13

14

15

16

17

Notes

(21–25) What purpose do the graphic details in this account of Eglon's death serve?

18

19

20

21

22

23

Notes

24

25

26

27

28

Notes

(30) In what way did the judges bring temporary rest to God's people?

(31) Was Shamgar an Israelite?

29

30

31

Notes

(1) What is the consistent pattern of Israel's apostasy?

(2–3) How does the revelation of God's wrath in Israel relate to that of the new covenant era (see Rom. 1:18–32)?

(4) What is a prophetess (see Ex. 15:20; 2 Kings 22:14; Neh. 6:14; Isa. 8:3)?

(6–7) What is Deborah calling Barak to do? Why didn't she want to lead the military herself?

Judges 4:1-6

1

2

3

4

5

6

Notes

(8–10) What is the result of Barak's hesitancy?

7

8

9

10

11

12

Notes

(14–15) Who is the ultimate warrior and victor in this account?

(17–22) What are the similarities and differences between Sisera's and Eglon's deaths (see Judg. 3:19–25)?

13

14

15

16

17

Notes

18

19

20

21

22

Notes

(23–24) Who was bringing about this defeat of Jabin—God or Israel? What does this indicate about the relationship between God's sovereignty and man's responsibility?

23

24

Notes

(1) Why should God's deliverances of His people lead them to praise Him with song? How does experiencing God's salvation lead to worship (see Ex. 15:1–21; Rom. 11:33–36)?

(3) How does a person's praise to God exhort the rest of the congregation (see Eph. 5:19)?

(4–5) What is God's march from Seir and Edom referring to? Why would Deborah include this in her song (see Deut. 33:2)?

(6–8) How is Deborah portrayed here?

Judges 5:1-8

1

2

3

4

5

6

7

8

Notes

(11) Who was to declare the mighty salvation that God had wrought?

(14–18) Which tribes participated in the battle against Jabin? Which ones did not respond to the call to take up arms?

9

10

11

12

13

14

Notes

(20–21) What is meant by natural elements (stars and torrent) fighting against the Canaanites?

15

16

17

18

19

20

21

Notes

(23–27) What is the reason for the stark contrast between the curse on Meroz and the blessing on Jael?

22

23

24

25

26

27

Notes

(28–30) Why would Deborah include this picture of Sisera's mother awaiting her son's return?

(31) How does one become a friend of God who truly loves Him?

28

29

30

31

Notes

(1) What is "evil"?

(2–6) God often brings about bitter providences as chastisement for sin. How do we determine whether such difficulties are the consequences of specific sins or not?

Judges 6:1-5

1

2

3

4

5

Notes

(8) Why would God send a prophet instead of a judge in response to Israel's cry?

(9) How was Israel's enslavement to Egypt similar to their plight under Midian?

(10) How does God's past deliverance of Israel serve to show the folly of their sin against Him?

(11) Why would Gideon beat out wheat in a winepress?

6

7

8

9

10

11

Notes

(12) Why would the Angel of the Lord begin by reminding Gideon of God's presence with him? From an earthly perspective, did it appear that God was with His people?

(13) Is Gideon's doubt valid? How should believers respond when their experience seems contrary to God's word?

(15) Why does God often choose the weakest and most unlikely of figures to carry out His purposes?

(16) How does God compensate for Gideon's weakness? How is this a comfort to you in your weakness?

12

13

14

15

16

17

Notes

(22) Why was Gideon fearful for his life? What does this indicate about the Angel of the Lord?

18

19

20

21

22

23

Notes

(24) Why would Gideon name the altar Jehovah-shalom—"The LORD is Peace"?

(27) What was Gideon's reason for waiting until evening to decimate Israel's idols?

24

25

26

27

28

Notes

(30) Who are the people seeking to kill Gideon?

(31–32) What did Joash's words and Gideon's new name reveal about the false god Baal?

(34) How does the work of the Spirit under the old covenant compare to His work under the new?

29

30

31

32

33

34

Notes

(37) Is Gideon's request for a sign a good model for all believers to confirm the will of God?

35

36

37

38

39

40

Notes

(2) What is the temptation for Israel?
Why is boasting in itself such a snare?

(3) Why would God target those who are fearful as the first to go (see Deut. 20:5–8)?

(4–8) What is God teaching Israel through the reduction of Gideon's army (see Zech. 4:6)?

Judges 7:1-5

1

2

3

4

5

Notes

(10–14) How does God fit Gideon's hands for battle and drive out his fear? What does this reveal about God?

6

7

8

9

10

Notes

(15) What is the relationship between Gideon's faith, worship, and obedience?

11

12

13

14

15

Notes

(16) What were the weapons wielded by Gideon's men? What was this intended to communicate (see 2 Cor. 10:4)?

(20) What is ironic about the war cry of Gideon?

16

17

18

19

20

Notes

(22) How does the Lord manifest His presence in the midst of the battle?

21

22

23

24

25

Notes

(1–3) How did Gideon display wisdom in his response to Ephraim's complaint?

(5–9) Who were the men of Succoth and Penuel? Was Gideon justified in his pronouncement of fierce threats toward them?

Judges 8:1-5

1

2

3

4

5

Notes

(10–12) Why is the presence of the Lord (so prominent in the previous chapter) not mentioned in Gideon's endeavors in this chapter?

6

7

8

9

10

11

Notes

(13–17) Is the representation of Gideon here positive or negative?

12

13

14

15

16

17

Notes

(18) What was motivating Gideon to pursue these Midianite kings?

(21) What was Gideon seeking to prove in killing Zebah and Zalmunna?

(22) What is the glaring omission in Israel's request?

(23) Is Gideon's response the result of a genuine humility before God or a facade of piety?

18

19

20

21

22

23

Notes

(24–27) What was an ephod? What does this act of Gideon reveal about his heart and the hearts of the people?

24

25

26

27

28

Notes

(30–31) What was the difference between a wife and a concubine?

(34) What happens when Israel fails to remember God and His deliverances? How could this apply to your own life?

29

30

31

32

33

34

35

Notes

(1) What set Abimelech apart from Gideon's seventy other sons (see Judg. 8:31)?

(2–3) What arguments does Abimelech use to sway Shechem to follow him and eventually make him king (see v. 6)?

(4–5) What do Abimelech's actions reveal about his character?

Judges 9:1-5

1

2

3

4

5

Notes

(7) Why is it significant that Jotham is pronouncing curses from Mount Gerizim (see Josh. 8:30–35)?

6

7

8

9

10

11

12

Notes

(8–15) What is the point of Jotham's parable? Is it condemning Abimelech or the Shechemites?

(16–19) What would have been the proper response of the Shechemites to Jotham's rebuke?

13

14

15

16

17

18

(20) What is the nature of the curse spoken against Abimelech and Shechem (see v. 15)?

(23–24) What does God bring about between Abimelech and the Shechemites? May God use evil spirits to accomplish His purposes (see 1 Sam. 13:13–16)?

19

20

21

22

23

24

Notes

(26–33) Who was Gaal? How is he a manifestation of the righteous judgment of God against Abimelech?

25

26

27

28

29

Notes

(34–54) How did these events fulfill the curse of Jotham pronounced on Mount Gerizim in verse 20?

30

31

32

33

34

35

Notes

36

37

38

39

40

41

Notes

42

43

44

45

46

47

Notes

48

49

50

51

52

53

Notes

(56–57) What is the author's conclusion of this account? What did he mean to teach Israel? What does it teach us today?

54

55

56

57

Notes

(1–5) Why are the accounts of Tola and Jair so brief in comparison to those of the other judges?

(6) God had demonstrated, especially through Gideon, the powerlessness of Baal. Why would the Israelites continue to fall prey to Baal worship after such mighty demonstrations of God's power and deliverance?

Judges 10:1-7

1

2

3

4

5

6

7

Notes

(10) What does Israel's cry to God indicate about their confidence in the Baals for deliverance?

(11–12) How does God's past grace highlight the devastating nature of Israel's bondage to the Philistines and the Ammonites?

8

9

10

11

12

13

Notes

(14) How is the righteousness of God manifested in this act of divine judgment?

(16) What does it mean for God to become grieved over Israel's impoverished state? Can God experience grief?

14

15

16

17

18

Notes

(1) How does the narrator describe Jephthah? What is the significance of this description?

(2) Why did Jephthah's brothers force him to leave his father's house?

(4–6) Why did the people of Gilead bring Jephthah back from Tob?

1

2

3

4

5

6

Notes

(7–9) What is Jephthah's response to the elders of Gilead? What does this indicate about his character?

(10–11) Why is the Lord's presence mentioned twice at the commissioning of Jephthah?

(12–13) Why are the Ammonites setting themselves against Israel?

7

8

9

10

11

12

Notes

(15–20) How did this record of Israel's history counter the request of the king of Ammon?

13

14

15

16

17

18

Notes

(21—23) Why did the land belong to Israel? How does Jephthah's response indicate his faith in God?

19

20

21

22

23

Notes

(24) Who is Chemosh? Why does Jephthah mention him here (see 1 Kings 11:7)?

(26) What is the significance of the three hundred years? What point is Jephthah making?

(27) Where does Jephthah's confidence lie? What relevance does this have for Christians today?

24

25

26

27

28

Notes

(29–30) What is the relationship between the Spirit coming upon Jephthah and Jephthah's vow?

(30–31) What exactly did Jephthah vow? Should Christians make vows today?

29

30

31

32

33

Notes

(35) Is Jephthah's unwillingness to break his vow commendable and honoring to God?

(36–37) What is the character of Jephthah's daughter?

(38–40) What happened to Jephthah's daughter as a result of his vow?

34

35

36

37

38

Notes

39

40

Notes

(1) Why are the men of Ephraim upset with Jephthah (see Judg. 8:1–3)?

(2–3) Is Ephraim's anger appropriate and justified?

(4) What does this civil war indicate about the condition of Israel?

Judges 12:1-5

1

2

3

4

5

Notes

(6) What are the men of Ephraim unable to do?

(9) What is the distinguishing characteristic of Ibzan? How does this contrast with Jephthah?

6

7

8

9

10

11

12

13

Notes

14

15

Notes

(1) Is God's judgment here characterized by wrath or fatherly chastisement?

(2) Why does God often use barren wombs to bring about His deliverance (see Gen. 17:15–22; Luke 1:5–25).

(3) Where else in Scripture does an angel announce a child's birth?

(5) What is a Nazirite? What are the rules Nazirites are required to keep (see Numbers 6)?

(6) Why does Manoah's wife call the Angel of the Lord "a man of God"?

Judges 13:1-6

1

2

3

4

5

6

Notes

(8–12) What does Manoah's response indicate about his spiritual state?

7

8

9

10

11

12

Notes

(18) How does the Angel describe His name? What is His point?

13

14

15

16

17

18

Notes

(20–22) Who does the Angel of the Lord reveal Himself to be (see Judg. 6:22)?

(24–25) Why does the narrator give such a detailed account of Samson's conception and birth, especially because his account of the last three judges was so brief (see Judg. 12:8–15)?

Judges 13:19-24

19

20

21

22

23

24

Notes

(25) What does it mean for the Spirit of God to "stir" or "move upon" Samson?

25

Notes

(2) Is Samson's demand respectful of his father's role and authority?

3) What is wrong with Samson's desire? How does he reflect Israel during this period? See Judges 17:6; 18:1; 19:1.

(4) God had made clear to the Israelites that they were not to marry unbelievers from foreign nations (Ex. 34:16: Deut. 7:3). How could Samson's marriage with a Philistine be "of the Lord?

1

2

3

4

5

Notes

(6) Why does the Spirit of God come upon Samson?

(8–9) Why doesn't Samson tell his parents where he got the honey from? Did he break his Nazirite vow in some way? How?

(11) Who are these thirty companions?

6

7

8

9

10

11

Notes

(16) With whom does the allegiance of Samson's wife lie?

12

13

14

15

16

Notes

(18) Why does Samson mention a heifer in his response to the Philistines? What does he mean by this?

(20) Who gave Samson's wife to his companion (see Judg. 15:2)?

Judges 14:17-20

17

18

19

20

Notes

(1) Why would Samson bring a young goat when he visits his wife?

(3–6) How did God use Samson's marriage to bring judgment on the Philistines?

Judges 15:1-5

1

2

3

4

5

Notes

(7) Is Samson's vengeance justified? Is there ever a time when Christians should seek retribution?

(8) What does it mean for Samson to strike the Philistines "hip and thigh"?

(11–13) Why would the men of Judah bind their own judge? What does this reveal about the power of the Philistines?

6

7

8

9

10

11

Notes

(14) Why does the narrator keep stressing the role of the Spirit in the deliverances brought about by Israel's judges?

(15) Why would a fresh jawbone of a donkey be a choice weapon?

12

13

14

15

16

17

Notes

(18–19) What is this account of Samson's thirst intended to teach us about Samson and about God?

18

19

20

Judges 16:1-6

1

2

3

4

5

6

Notes

(7–14) What are the three lies that Samson tells Delilah about the source of his strength? How does each serve to mock the Philistines?

7

8

9

10

11

12

Notes

(15–17) How is this account connected to that of Judges 14:17? What does this teach us about the nature of temptation and the need to flee from it?

Judges 16:13-17

13

14

15

16

17

Notes

(20) What was the true source of Samson's strength?

(21) How might the gouging out of Samson's eyes be directly connected to his lustful disposition (see Judg. 14:1–3; 16:1)?

(22) Why would the narrator mention Samson's hair growing?

Judges 16:18-22

18

19

20

21

22

Notes

(23–24) How was this a reversal of God's original intention in raising up Samson as judge?

23

24

25

26

27

Notes

(28) What does this petition reveal about Samson's heart (see Heb. 11:32–38)?

(30) Samson strikes a massive blow to the Philistines in his death. In what ways is this similar to the death of Christ? In what ways is it different? Can Samson rightly be called a type of Christ?

28

29

30

31

Notes

(1) Why does the narrator shift from a narrative about the judges to stories about more common people like Micah?

(2) What does this narrative tell us about the characters of Micah and his mother?

(3) What is the irony in what Micah's mother does?

(5) What laws of the old covenant was Micah violating?

(6) How is Micah's sin related to that of the entire nation?

Judges 17:1-6

1

2

3

4

5

6

Notes

(7) Was Bethlehem one of the cities given to the Levites to dwell in (see Josh. 21:9–40)?

(9) What was the God-ordained task of the Levites?

(10–12) What appears to be the Levite's motive in serving Micah this way?

Judges 17:7-12

7

8

9

10

11

12

Notes

(13) What is Micah's motive in hiring the Levite?

13

Notes

(1) Why had no inheritance been given to the tribe of Dan (see Judg. 1:34–35)?

(3) How were the Danites able to recognize the Levite?

(6) Why would the Levite respond in such vague generalities?

Judges 18:1-6

1

2

3

4

5

6

Notes

(7–13) Are the Danites acting in faith as they seek to take possession of the land?

7

8

9

10

11

Notes

(17) What do the actions of the Danites reveal about their view of God?

12

13

14

15

16

17

Notes

(20) What was wrong with the heart of this Levite? How can you be tempted to do religious things for selfish gain rather than for the glory of God?

18

19

20

21

22

23

Notes

(24) How does Micah exemplify the tragedy of idolatry?

24

25

26

27

28

Notes

(30) What is revealed about the lineage of the Levite (see Ex. 2:22)? What would this have taught the original readers?

(30) What is the captivity spoken of here (see 2 Kings 15:29)? What does this indicate about the time in which Judges was authored?

29

30

31

Notes

(1) Why does the author keep stating that there is no king in Israel? How would having a king change Israel's situation?

(2) Is the role of a concubine morally acceptable to God?

(4–9) How does the hospitality shown by this man's father-in-law contrast with the hospitality he would later encounter in Gibeah (see vv. 15–26)?

1

2

3

4

5

Notes

(10–12) Why wouldn't the man spend the night in Jebus? What is the irony?

6

7

8

9

10

Notes

(16) Why is it significant that the man who showed hospitality to the Levite was an outsider?

11

12

13

14

15

16

Notes

17

18

19

20

21

Notes

(22–26) How does this situation parallel that of Sodom in Genesis 19:4–9? What does this indicate about Israel?

22

23

24

25

26

Notes

(29) What is the purpose of this shocking and repulsive action?

27

28

29

30

Notes

(1–2) Why is the entire nation of Israel assembling together?

1

2

3

4

5

Notes

(6) In light of Israel's pervasive immorality, what made the sin of Gibeah worth fighting over?

(8–11) How did the nation respond to Gibeah's wickedness?

6

7

8

9

10

11

Notes

(13) What is the reason for wanting to put to death the men of Gibeah?

(16) What would be beneficial about being a left-handed warrior?

12

13

14

15

16

17

Notes

(18) Why would God choose Judah to be the first to fight?

(19–26) What was God teaching Israel in allowing them to be defeated by the Benjaminites?

18

19

20

21

22

23

Notes

(27–28) Who was Phinehas? What was the significance of him ministering before the ark (see Num. 25:6–11)?

24

25

26

27

28

29

Notes

30

31

32

33

34

Notes

(35) Who defeated Benjamin--God or Israel? What does this teach us about God's sovereignty and man's responsibility?

(36–46) What was Israel's battle strategy?

35

36

37

38

39

Notes

40

41

42

43

44

45

Notes

(47–48) Was the tribe of Benjamin completely wiped out?

46

47

48

Notes

(1) When was this oath taken by the Israelites?

(2–3) What is the cause for Israel's mourning in the face of military victory?

(4) Why is Israel offering up sacrifices to God?

1

2

3

4

5

6

Notes

(7) Subsequent to the civil war, what problem does the tribe of Benjamin face?

(8–12) What is Israel's justification for wiping out Jabesh Gilead and taking the virgins therein? Was this a proper response?

7

8

9

10

11

Notes

12

13

14

15

16

17

Notes

(18) Why doesn't Israel simply undo their oath?

(19–23) How does this narrative expose the immorality of God's covenant people?

18

19

20

21

22

Notes

(25) How does Israel's apostasy anticipate the need for a godly king?

23

24

25

The Book of

Ruth

Notes

(1) During what period did Ruth enter redemptive history? What was Israel's spiritual condition at this time (see Judg. 2:11–13)?

(1–2) What was the reason for these Israelites living in Moab?

(3–5) Apart from the sorrow of bereavement, why was it tragic in ancient times for a woman to lose her husband and sons?

(4) What is the potential danger of marrying Moabite women (see Deut. 7:1–3)?

(5) If you had experienced the trials that Naomi does here, how would you be tempted to perceive God?

(6) What is Naomi's basis for going back to her hometown? How is her returning a picture of repentance?

Ruth 1:1-6

1

2

3

4

5

6

Notes

(8–9) What does Naomi's statement toward her daughters-in-law indicate about her character? Why would she send them away?

(11) Why would Naomi mention her womb?

7

8

9

10

11

12

Notes

(13) How does Naomi view God's relation to her? Is her view of God correct?

(15–17) What did Ruth commit to Naomi? What is the religious significance of this commitment?

13

14

15

16

17

18

Notes

(19) Bethlehem means "house of bread." Why is its name ironic in this story?

(20) What do the names Naomi and Mara mean?

(21) How does the Lord providentially govern the bitter and painful events in the lives of His people?

(22) Why does the narrator continue emphasizing that Ruth is a Moabite?

19

20

21

22

Notes

(1) What does this verse tell us about Boaz?

(2) What provisions had God made in the law for the poor and widowed to gather food (see Lev. 19:9–10; Deut. 24:19)?

(3) Why would the narrator say that Ruth just happened to stumble upon the field of Boaz? Is this a random event?

(4) In the midst of a godless age, what does Boaz's greeting indicate about his spiritual condition?

1

2

3

4

5

6

Notes

(9) How was Boaz's command for the men not to touch Ruth rooted in God's law (see Deut. 22:25–27).

(10) Why is Ruth so overwhelmed by the grace Boaz shows to her? How is this similar to the response Christians should have to the grace of Christ?

7

8

9

10

11

Notes

(12) What is the imagery of God used by Boaz here (see Ps. 36:7; 91:4)?

(14–16) How does Boaz's kindness toward Ruth exceed the statutes of the law?

(17) How much is an ephah of barley? Approximately how long would this have lasted Ruth and Naomi?

12

13

14

15

16

17

Notes

(20) Who extends the kindness referred to by Naomi--God or Boaz?

18

19

20

21

22

Notes

(23) How long was a typical harvest time?

23

Notes

(1) What does Naomi mean by "rest" (or "security") here (see Ruth 1:8; 4:13)?

(2) What was the purpose of a threshing floor? How does John the Baptist use it as a metaphor (see Matt. 3:12)?

(4) Why would Naomi instruct Ruth to lie down at Boaz's feet?

Ruth 3:1-6

1

2

3

4

5

6

Notes

(9) How does the imagery here harken back to Boaz's prayer in Ruth 2:12?

(10) How was Ruth showing kindness to Boaz?

(12) In this verse, Boaz takes on the role of a kinsman-redeemer. What would it entail for Boaz to redeem Ruth?

7

8

9

10

11

12

Notes

(14) Why would Boaz not want it to be known that Ruth had visited the threshing floor?

(17) How does Boaz function as God's means of blessing to Ruth and Naomi?

13

14

15

16

17

Notes

18

Notes

(1) In ancient Israel, what was the significance of the town gate?

(2) Why were the elders invited to sit down with Boaz and the close relative (also called a kinsman and a redeemer)? (See Deuteronomy 21:19; 22:15; 25:7.)

(3–4) Why would Boaz and the close relative care if Naomi is selling land (see Lev. 25:25)?

(5–6) Why did the close relative decide not to redeem Naomi's estate?

Ruth 4:1-5

1

2

3

4

5

Notes

(8) What was the significance of removing one sandal?

(8–10) In what way(s) does Boaz point to Christ?

6

7

8

9

10

Notes

(11) How was Ruth used to build up the house of Israel? What is the significance of God accomplishing this through a Moabite?

(13) Who enables Ruth to become pregnant? Why is this significant?

(14–17) How did the Lord reverse Naomi's bitter and empty situation, which she lamented in Ruth 1:20–21?

Ruth 4:11-16

11

12

13

14

15

16

Notes

(18–22) What is the messianic significance of this closing genealogy (see Isa. 11:10; Rom. 1:3; Rev. 22:16)?

17

18

19

20

21

22

Notes

Notes

Notes

Notes

Notes